For Nathan, Audrey, and Isaac

My Dad has Bipolar I

Written and Illustrated by Krista Morgan Eger

Hi my name is Nate. This is my Dad.
He has Bipolar Disorder.

This disorder is in his brain, so sometimes he acts
different than usual.

Sometimes he acts really happy and excited.

Sometimes he acts really sad.

And sometimes he quickly switches back and forth between happy and mad.

That's because my dad's brain is different.

There's a part of our brains called the Limbic System. It turns on when we feel angry, excited, or scared.

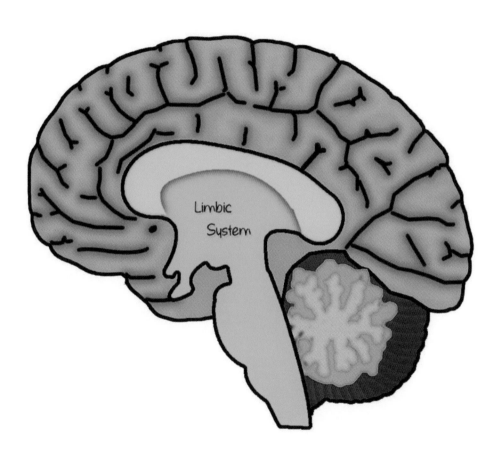

When our brain is healthy, the limbic system only turns on when we need it to. When it is off, we feel calm and we can solve problems more easily.

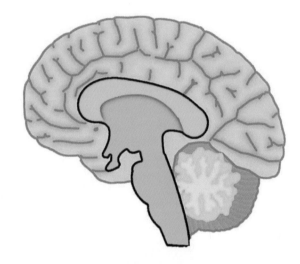

-Alert
-Ready to Fight or Run
-Scared
-Excitable

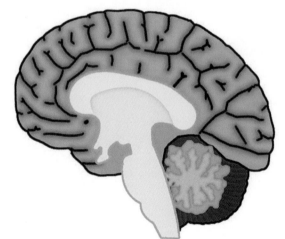

-Calm
-Content
-Solve Problems
-Complete Daily Tasks

The limbic system signals our bodies to release a chemical called adrenaline. Its job is to make feelings stronger or more intense.

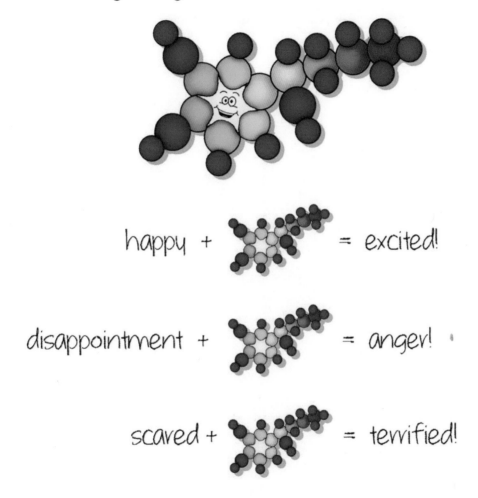

happy + = excited!

disappointment + = anger!

scared + = terrified!

Roller coasters are fun because our body releases adrenaline that makes our happy feelings stronger.

Our limbic system can be tricky. Sometimes the feelings it gives us are so strong, they feel true. Think of how you feel when you are really mad at someone. Have you ever felt like you would always be mad at them and it would never go away? But when you calm down and they apologize, you're not mad at them anymore.

In that moment of anger when you felt like you would never stop being mad at them, didn't it feel real?

My dad has bipolar 1. This type of bipolar causes him to have episodes called mania and hypomania. When this happens, his limbic system turns up and *won't* turn down.

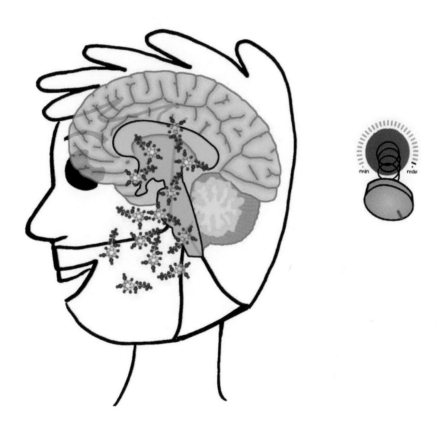

Every feeling he has is stronger because his body has too much adrenaline.

Every feeling is so strong that it feels real to him.

Sometimes he says things that are really confusing. Like when he says we can go somewhere really fun, but we never go.

Sometimes he gets mad at me and I don't know what I did wrong.

When my dad has an episode, I feel:

Scared

Hurt

Disappointed

Angry

Sad

It's ok to feel all these feelings if one of your parents has bipolar too. You're not alone.

I know it's not my dad's fault or my fault he acts this way. Now he goes to the doctor and therapist so that he can get better and stay better. I know he will do the best he can because most of all, I know he loves me.

And I love him too!

Bipolar Disorder is a complex mood disorder. This book is a simplified version to help children of parents who live with the disorder understand what is going on instead of internalizing their parent's behavior. To learn more about the disorder and understand its true complexity, please consider the following sources:

Madness: A Bipolar Life by Marya Hornbacher

An Unquiet Mind: A Memoir of Moods and Madness by Kay Redfield Jamison

Bipolar for Dummies by Candida Fink and Joe Kraynak

Loving Someone with Bipolar Disorder by Julie A. Fast

National Institute of Mental Health
https://www.nimh.nih.gov/health/publications/bipolar-disorder/index.shtml

Depression and Bipolar Support Alliance
www.DBSAlliance.org

National Alliance for the Mentally Ill
www.nami.org

This book was inspired by a conversation I had with my son Nathan while my husband was in an inpatient facility recovering from a manic episode. Seeing him understand his dad in a new way and hearing the relief in his voice inspired me to create this children's book for other kids going through the same thing. The people pictured in this book are real people. Thank you for taking the time to read our story.

-Krista Morgan Eger

Printed in Great Britain
by Amazon

18682315R20016